Contents

	Page
Preface	
Indian Terracotta Art	1
History of Indian Terracottas	11
Terracotta in Bengal	13
Plates	
Notes on the Plates	I—X

Evamiva hi yosam
Prsamsanti—prithu-sronih
Vimristantaramsa, madhye
Samgrahyeti

       (*Sata-Bramhana, 1, 2, 5, 16*)

'Thus they praise a woman who
is broad-hipped, of smooth breast region
and slender-waisted'

Preface

The most ancient and original form of expression of plastic art was through the medium of terracottas. But, subsequently, due to certain obvious disadvantages it became the vernacular form of expression in all parts of the land excepting the East, where it flourished to a great extent, where stone could not be hauled owing to lack of transport facilities.

But, inspite of these factors, we find here and there—all over this vast sub-continent—a continuous stream of specimens of terracotta art throughout all the different ages of our cultural tradition. They have their own characteristic features and the particular trend is distinctively prominent everywhere.

But due to its fragile quality mostly all the worthwhile specimens have disintegrated and the remaining few have become museum pieces and I think those very few glittering monuments, profusely decorated with terracotta plaques and medallions, which we still see all over the Eastern India, will not survive the vagaries of weather for a long time unless they are properly looked after.

Looking through the collection of pictures arranged here, I must admit, and I believe that my readers will also agree with me, that side by side with other branches of plastic art Indian terracottas have contributed to a large extent to enrich our cultural heritage. Previously we did very little to evaluate the creative and aesthetic merit of *Indian Terracotta Art* and I shall regard my efforts quite successful if this small monograph serves the purpose of creating some amount of inspiration in the mind of our young scholars, who will try to explore more about this branch of creative art in the near future.

In this venture I owe a great deal to my friend Sri Amiya Tarafdar for his fine work and to my friend Mr. George Wittenborn of America and his charming wife Joyce for their valuable suggestions during all the stages of production of this volume.

I also express my indebtedness to the Archaeological Department for allowing me to use a few pictures from their collection and to Sri Aurobindo Ghosh for helping me to compile the notes.

Calcutta, the 15th April, 1959   A. Goswami

Indian Terracotta Art

TERRACOTTAS ('baked clay') are the vernacular medium of figural sculpture in all early cultures, in World's Art—in Minos and Ancient Greece, in Egypt, Iran and Mesopotamia, in China, Polynesia and in Pre-Columbian American Art, providing surprising forms of beauty in naive and primitive expressions,—which have challenged lovers and connoisseurs of art and curators of Museums, anxious to pay any prices for these delightfully tiny toys of clay, which, sometimes, have stood for images of mysterious religious beliefs of grave spiritual import.

Sir Arthur Evans unearthed wonderful clay figurines of surpassing beauty, examples of Pre-Hellenic Art, from his excavations of the Palace of Minos at Knossos in the island of Crete, datable between 1700 and 1600 B.C. The great masterpiece of Minoan Terracotta is the world-famous figure of two women, seated on rectangular chairs opposite each other, and deeply engaged in spinning and eagerly conversing,—a veritable epic of domestic life, in many ways surpassing the beauty of ambitious marbles and bronzes. In Cyprus, the farthest of the Greek islands close to the Near East, a Swedish expedition discovered in this ancient cradle of a unique culture-complex, an enormous quantity of more than 2000 pieces of archaic terracottas (some of life-size) at an undisturbed temple-site near the village of Ajia Irini.

In Continental Greece, from about the 5th century B.C., terracotta statuettes have been produced in enormous quantities at two centres, at Tanagra, a small town of Boetia, and at Eretria in the island of Euboea, which in their charm, grace and humour have winned the hearts of connoisseurs away from the great masterpieces in marbles and bronzes and which have now filled the show-cases of all the museums of the world. While the marbles and bronzes cover the imaginary world of the Greek Olympus, the terracottas of Greece illustrate the common life of Greece in her secular and domestic occupations,—yet, the majority of these tiny statuettes were votive offerings to the temples and shrines. These offerings were made not only by grown-ups and adults, but also by young boys and maidens. Sometimes these votive offerings were accompanied by dedicatory inscriptions and epigrams, one of which we are tempted to cite here, an epigram from a maiden named Timarete:

> 'To Artemis : Maiden, to thee, before her marriage Timarete gives
> Her cap, her tambourines, her favourite ball,
> And as is meet, Oh ! Artemis, the maiden brings
> Her childhood's toys, her dolls, their clothes and all.'

Another epigram is very tense and terse in its expression :

> 'This little toy was mighty Brutus' pet,
> Great its renown, though small the statuette.'

It is well-known that the temple guardians periodically emptied the shrines under their charge of the votive offerings which had accumulated there ; some of the metal objects were melted down and made into basins and furniture for the temple service, but nothing could be done with the terracotta figures or vases, so they were thrown away ; but to prevent the desecration of objects which had belonged to a divinity, they were first broken. In all such collections, there are broadly speaking, two classes of clay figures—those which have some obvious connection with temple worship and those which have not. "The relative proportions of these two groups vary considerably, and if we take the finds at two Greek temple-sites, the shrine of Demeter and Kore at Tegea in the Peloponnessos and the temple of Athene Kraneia at Elataea in Northern Greece, we obtain the following results. At Tegea, two hundred figures of the local goddesses, five hundred water-carriers (temple-attendants) and a number of pigs (sacrificial animals); at Elataea only eight statuettes of Athene and twenty-two of other divinities, eighteen dancing figures (temple-attendants) and one of a priestess bearing a pig" (Hutton : Greek Terracotta Statuettes, 1899, p. 3). The most charming of the Greek terracottas are the types of Greek ladies in outdoor dresses, wearing curious hats. These fully-draped figures contrast, in their dignity and poses, with the nude forms of the famous Gods in marble. The terracottas now form one of the most brilliant chapters of Greek Art.

In Egypt, in all periods of its art-history from the Proto-Dynastic period (5650-4777 B. C.) to the Ptolemaic Period (331-30 B. C.), terracotta figurines have been made in abundance as parallel plastic efforts to the great monumental sculptures in stone, bronze and wood. In Egypt, terracotta figurines did not illustrate votive purposes or religious beliefs, but were the most fluent and easy medium to record the secular life in all phases of domestic living. In the museum at Cairo, there are realistic representations of domestic scenes and occupations—not only in groups but in lively realistic types. Thus, we have groups of bakers kneading breads, scenes in cook-room, filled with cooks and attendants in diverse branches of cooking. Another lively group in the same museum is a picture of fine musicians engaged in a concert. Interesting types are servants carrying baggages of their masters and long rows of carriers (in groups of two abreast) taking offerings to the temples. More formidable groups are representations of light and heavy infantries in solemn military march. A well-known masterpiece is the study of a type, a seated cook, excellently posed in a contemplative mood. Interesting animal studies are camels and elephants. The best contributions in Egyptian terracottas are several grotesque heads, rendered with amusing dexterity, sometimes with obscene suggestions. In a famous stele, a famous artist named Sen-irui records his own qualification. He calls himself 'a craftsman, excellent in his craft, and supreme in his knowledge'. We should refer here to a very significant example of a terracotta Nude Goddess from Egypt. It is a marvellous figure of remarkable beauty posed in a significant gesture, with her arms raised above her head—with a peculiar head in the shape of a hook—with no attempt to put on the face any manner of expression, which is confined to the gesture of the arms, stretched out and raised over the head intended to emphasize invitingly her bare breasts, the emphatic symbols of her motherhood. Basically, it stands for the Earth Goddess, with significant analogies with the types from Mesopotamia (Elam and other sites) and from India, which will be discussed later. This piece of polychrome terracotta, 10½ inches high, belongs to Pre-Dynastic Egypt and is datable in about 5000 B.C., having come to the Brooklyn Museum (U.S.A.) from the Museum's own excavations in upper Egypt in 1907 (Art News, Summer 1957, p. 44).

Before we allude to terracottas of the Near-Eastern culture-areas, we should cite the very interesting productions of the early American Tribal culture of the Pre-Columbian era. The ceramic figurines of Pre-Columbian Mexico are among the most fascinating products of the Middle-American Culture. "Because of the nature of the material from which they are made, the ease with which it can be handled and the resulting freedom it offers the artist, these objects are very valuable in affording a clear insight into the most basic of cultural traits, namely, the customary mode of expression. In this respect, they are probably of greater value than the more impressive monuments of stone" (E. G. Jackson, San Diego State College Bulletin). From the Lake Chapala regions and from the state of Nayarit (Mexico) have come wonderfully posed seated Men and Women, and some 'Mother and Child' effigies, which are veritable masterpieces of primitive culture. These eloquent types are intended to be naturalistic and they represent the every-day life of the people. Men, Women and Children are shown in all positions, and the forms appear to have been modelled with complete confidence. The makers of these figurines were actually keen observers and their works are full of life and truth.

We now come to some of the baked clay products of pre-historic times in West-Asiatic regions. Excavations, on behalf of the University Museum of Philadelphia carried on at an ancient site called Tureng Tepe (12 miles north-east of Asterabad and 42 miles east of the south-east corner of the Caspian Sea) have yielded (besides a number of red ware pottery with black-painted decorations) an interesting series of clay figurines, either red or gray, effigies of nude males and females in a few fixed attitudes. The rendering of the head is primitive though forceful, with prominent nose, square chin and no mouth at all. Particular interest attaches to a number of naked female statuettes (about 25 cm. high) made of baked reddish brown clay, all very much alike, standing with the hands holding the breasts, probably connected with the worship of the Great Mother Goddess (Mater Greta) which was widespread in Western Asia throughout pre-historic ages. They have been ascribed by the excavator (Frederick R. Walsin) to the Bronze Age, roughly 2500 to 1200 B.C. (Bulletin of the American Institute for Persian Art and Archæology, March 1932). Particular interest attaches to a fine nude female figurine, with outstretched arms in a dramatic pose, the hands rendered in pointed shapes without any details of the fingers, but the wrists beautifully decorated with a series of bangles and the neck decorated with a necklace of 'seven strings' (*sat-nara*) in a series of descending curves, reaching between the breasts, each of the string being marked by a jewel. The narrow wasp-waist spreads below in rounded voluptuous buttocks, developing beautifully shaped thighs tapering to finely modelled legs. The Mount of Venus with pubic hairs is conspicuously indicated in the shape of a triangle covering the whole of the abdomen. There is no doubt, that the Mother Goddess is intended to be represented. The type is very nearly related to a small nude female figure, with the hands doubled up to touch the breasts, cited by Coomaraswamy and said to have come from the Peshwar District. The Indian type of Mother Goddess is, therefore, linked up with the Bronze Age figurine from Asterabad.

Another Near-Eastern site has yielded several significant examples of

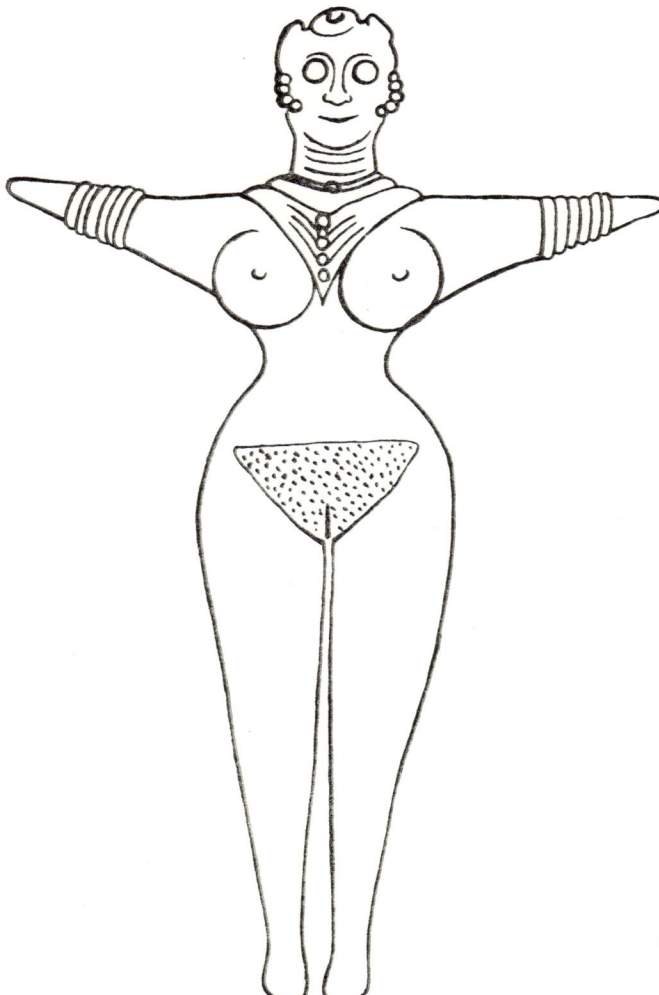

(b) Early Mediterranean Terracotta

(d) Earth-Goddess, Laurya, Nandangarh.

(a) Terracotta female figurine, Tureno Tepe near Asterabad.

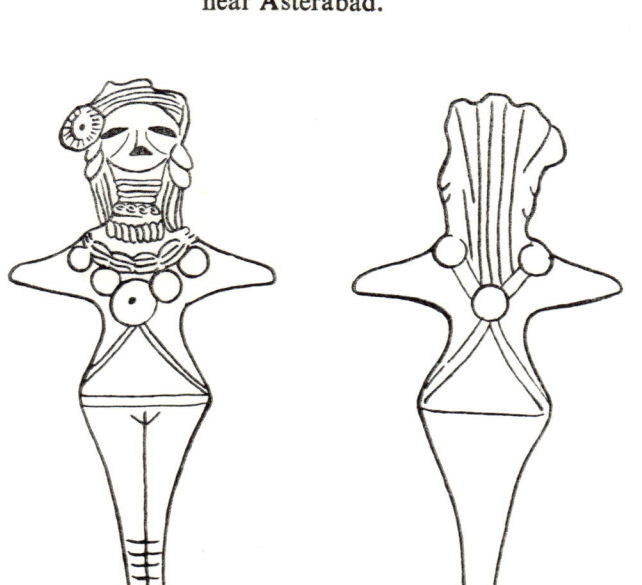

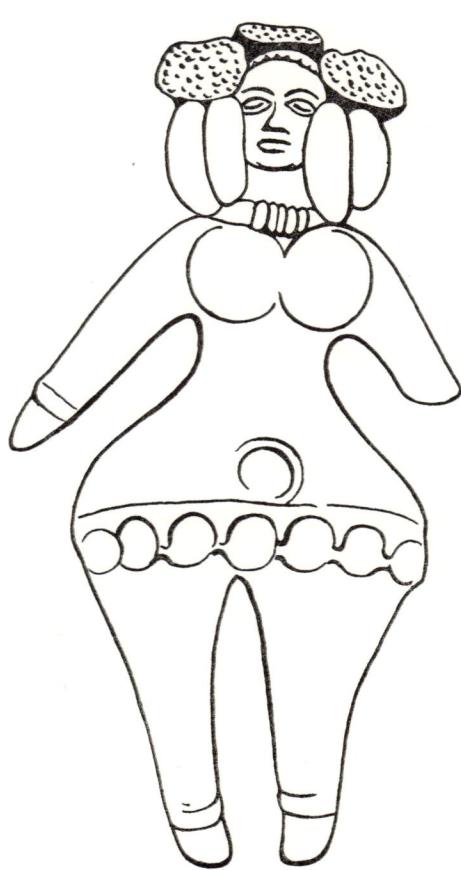

(c) Earth-Goddess, Mohenjo-daro.

(e) Earth-Goddess, Taxila (?)

terracotta figurines, representing the Nude Goddess. A French Archaeological Mission, organized by the Comite de L'Asia Francaise, in the course of excavations conducted in the year 1923, in the regions of Susa and Elam, the ancient sites of Babylonian culture, has brought to light a number of beautiful figurines of the cult of the Nude Goddess of great aesthetic and archaeological interest. The outstanding items are four pieces, two of which have been assigned to the early Babylonian Epoch (twentieth century Before Christ) and two have been ascribed to the Neo-Babylonian period (9th and 8th Century B.C.).

All the four figurines stand in similar attitude, with the feet closely set together and with the identical gesture of holding the breasts with their hands, a gesture symbolical of the Cult of Motherhood. So that it could be claimed that all of them are effigies of the Mother Goddess. Excepting one, all the other three are types revealing prominent buttocks, one of them formulated in a type with fantastically exaggerated buttocks, rendered in elaborate curves, which terminate in the narrow support of the legs and feet, closely held together. The luscious curves of the nether anatomy are artistically echoed by the rounded forms of the shoulders and arms. These echoing curves lend a quaint beauty and queer dignity to the figures worthy of a grave and mysterious cult-image. In one of the earlier figures, the hairs of the pubic region are indicated in the form of a cone made up of a series of dots, recalling similar treatment of the same feature in the figurine from Asterabad, cited above. In the other two examples, this feature develops into a peculiar ornament, consisting of rows of pearls (?) covering the whole of the waist above the Mount of Venus. The navel is indicated by a tiny dip. We are analysing the forms of this series of Nude Figurines with some details, as this will help us to link up the type with their Indian counterpart, to be cited later. The series of pearl ornaments round the waist approach very nearly the Indian conception of the jewellery, very well-known by the technical name of the *mekhala* (waist-band).

Analogous nude figurines, in red burnished clay, with hands clasping the breasts, have been dug up at a Chalcolithic site at Anatolia (Hacilar), which goes to suggest the wide geographical distribution of the Cult of the Mother Goddess (The Listner, No. 1511, 13th March 1958, pp. 445-46). Though not offering fruitful analogies in cult motives, the artistic treasures of Chinese terracottas are of great interest from many other points of view and as products of neighbourly sites separated from India by impenetrable mountain barriers, in the Buddhist periods, if not in the earlier periods of the Han, the clay figurines of China provide objects of absorbing study by virtue of their multiplicity of types and by the richly imaginative patterns and models of their plastic formulation, to which all the connoisseurs of the world have extended their unstinted admiration and praise.

The Chinese terracottas drew the attention of scholars and critics from the large amount of clay figurines dug up from ancient tombs from the Han Period (206 B.C. to 25 A.D.) which marks the beginning of an entirely new era in Chinese civilization. Oswald Siren, the great authority on Chinese Art, has made very significant comments on the Tomb satuettes of China, studied under two groups—Human Figures and Animal Forms: "It is only in the small clay statuettes that the Chinese attempt a more naturalistic treatment of the human figure, many of these are actually intended to represent living human beings, but even then, the artistic expression lies more in the linear delineation of the draperies than in the modelling of the form. These tomb statuettes form a group of their own outside the domain of the great sculpture" (Burlington Magazine monograph: Chinese Art, 1925, p. 47). A great part of the tomb statuettes consists of remarkable effigies of animals treated in a realistic manner and in significant graphic powers of delineation, principally illustrated in the representations of camels, horses, bulls and other domestic pets, presented in astonishingly naturalistic technique of superior artistic excellence. Typically characteristic effigies of camels and horses are to be seen in most of the museums of Europe and America. Oswald Siren's comments deserve to be quoted here: "The relatively inferior position of the

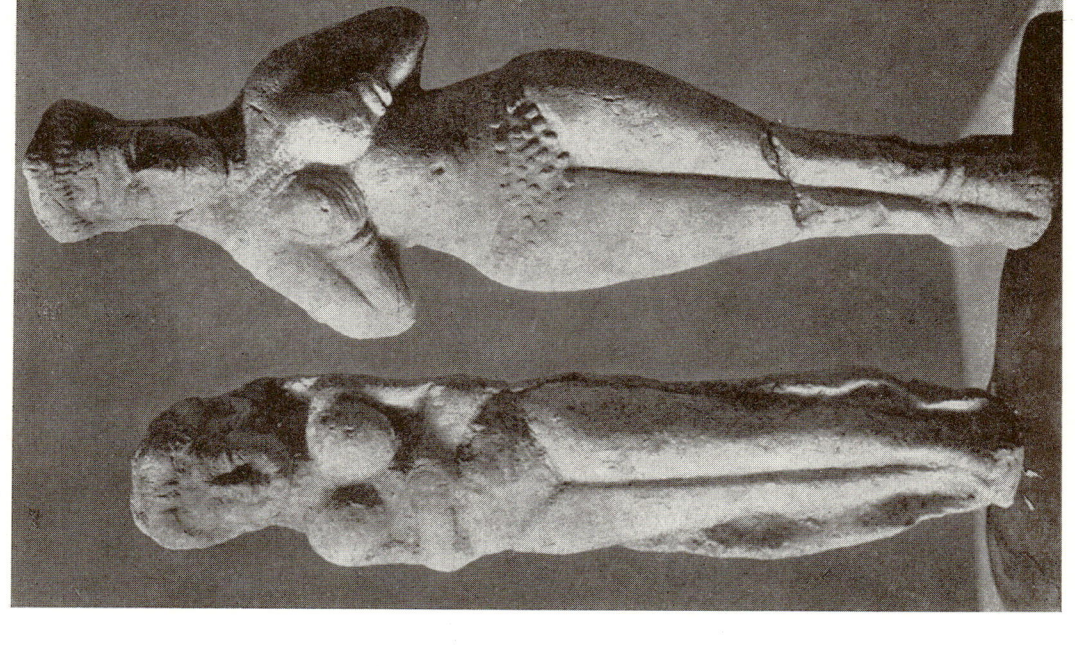

Neo-Babylonian Terracotta, 800 B.C.

Mother-Goddess, Elamite, 1100 B.C.

Early Terracotta from Babylon, 2000 B.C.

human figure in Chinese sculpture becomes most evident if one compares the religious statues, which form the bulk of the figure sculpture in China, with the representations of animals. The conventional restraint in the treatment of the bodily form and the strict adherence to traditional types, postures and motives of drapery which are so characteristic of most of the statues are scarcely to be found, or at least, not to the same degree in the animal sculptures. These sculptures are by no means abstract symbols, they may adhere to certain types of formulae characteristic of a period or province, but their artistic importance and expression depend mainly on the rendering of their organic form and vitality. The best among them are monumental creations hardly inferior to the animal sculptures of any other period or nation" (Ibid, p. 47).

The significance and purpose of the Tomb statuettes deserve some explanations. "From the earliest times the Chinese have been accustomed to place in their graves objects of beauty and rarity to help the dead on his new journey of life. It is not till Chou times that this custom of interring valuables was entirely given up and substitutes of base material (e. g. clay) used instead. These substitutes, known as *ming-chi* were made in great quantities, and it is in this connection that human figures in straw and clay were first used. Confucius disapproved of the use of wooden and clay figures with jointed limbs, as he considered them too human and the ceremony of their burial too much like immolation. For it must be remembered that till quite late in Chou times, people and animals were buried alive in the tombs of important people. Wu, prince of China, who died in 677 B.C. had sixty-six people buried with him. Confucius disapproved of this immolation, and it was perhaps as the result of his intervention that the custom of making pottery images become common" (Leigh Ashton: An Introduction to the Study of Chinese Sculpture, 1924, p. 13). Bernard Rackham has commented on the extraordinary level of aesthetic attainment of Chinese Terracotta: "Some are perhaps clumsy and ungainly, few have any special pretensions to be singled out as great masterpieces of art, but a very large proportion are entitled to the respect with which, when they were first revealed to us, they were hailed as works of uncommon power and distinction." More approximate relevance to the study of Indian terracotta is provided by the series of large size polychrome pottery statues of the Lohans of Buddhist significance, which have furnished monumental pieces to the gallery of Chinese sculpture. At least five pieces of these excellent masterpieces of pottery statues of Lohans are known—one in the British Museum, one in the Metropolitan Museum, New York, and another in the University Museum, Philadelphia. All of these have been assigned to the Tang Dynasty (618-905 A.D.). Others are in the Berlin Museum, in the Boston Museum, and in the Cleveland Museum. They are believed to have come from an old mountain sanctuary near Ichowfu, in Chihli (China), locally known as the Ba-fo-wa, Hill of the Eight Buddhas—implying that the number of effigies of Lohans, located in the sanctuary, was originally eight.

These remarkable pottery statues are supposed to be portraits of one or other of the sixteen Lohans, described in Buddhist Literature. They are wonderfully realistic representations, marked by individual and different gestures and postures for each portrait, particularly in the poses of the hands.

The British Museum specimen is eloquently described by R. L. Hobson in the following words: "A glance at our statue is sufficient to convince us that it belongs to a classic period of Chinese art. Its simplicity and grandeur, the directness with which it expresses the Buddhist ideal of deep contemplation and abstraction from earthly affairs belong to an age when the inspiration was fresh and the Buddhist art was young and virile and unstaled by conventions. So, too, the powerful modelling and the careful finish of the details are the work of a sculptor trained in the best school."

It is possible that models of these portraits of Lohans were originally derived from Indian Buddhist sources. And it is advisable to search amongst the numerous Buddhist sculptures in India, the original Indian prototype which might have provided inspiration to Chinese masters for fashioning these remarkable series of portraits of the Lohans.

History of Indian Terracottas

TERRACOTTA figurines in India, ranging over a period of three thousand years, belong to times, both before and after the use of stone for purposes of fashioning sculptural forms. It is permissible to believe that burnt clay was the common medium for cult-figurines before the use of stone became common, though this cheap and popular medium continued to be used for cult-worship long after stone came into common use.

The earliest examples of terracotta illustrate the cult of a Nude Goddess, which was at one time very wide-spread in all parts of West-Asiatic culture-sites—Sumer, Mesopotamia, ancient Iran and extending as far east as the Gangetic Valley. Most of these figurines of Nude Goddesses, characterised as Indo-Sumerian by Coomaraswamy, are dated tentatively in the second millennium B.C., thus attributed to Indus Valley culture of Mohenjo-Daro and Harappa. By an analysis of the details of the ornaments, particularly with reference to the girdle *(mekhala)*, Coomaraswamy has discovered a significant Vedic element in this group of Nude Goddesses.

Three specimens of these nude figurines (figs. a,b,c,—p.6) can be grouped as close analogous by reason of their common features—extended arms, exaggerated buttocks, deep navels (*nimna nabhi*), with nude body; with several items of jewellery—hairpins, ear-rings, necklaces, girdles and anklets. One of the figurines (fig. c) has in addition, a body ornament, consisting of a double-chain crossing fastened by a boss in front and behind. This ornament is known later as a *Channavira*. The most significant jewellery is the girdle, indicated by two incised lines (fig. c) and by a series of bosses linked together. This element is continued in a later representation of a nude goddess, on a gold plaque from Laurya, Nandangarh (fig. d) attributed to about 8th century B. C. The elegant figurine (fig. e) is said to have come possibly from Taxila, where many pre-Mayuryan terracottas have been found—the arms, now broken, appear to be folded across the breast, emphasizing and pointing out the motherhood of the icon, symbolized by the breast. In the other three figures, the hands are spread out in a gesture of affection. The girdle is also emphatic in the significance of a child-bearing fertility feature. The Atharva-Veda specified the girdle (*mekhala*) as a long life (*ayusyam*) charm. So, the series of nude figurines, all having girdles, may be recognized as a cult-image of Vedic affiliation. The Nude Goddess was also current in Aegean and other European culture-areas. And the significance of this cult is very well-interpreted by Glotz for the Aegean area, in the following terms :

"She is the Great Mother. It is she who makes all nature bring forth. All existing things are emanations from her. She is the madonna carrying the holy child, or watching over him. She is the mother of men and of animals, too. She continually appears with an escort of beasts, for she is the mistress of wild animals, snakes, birds and fishes. She even makes the plants grow by her universal fecundity, perpetuating the vegetative force of which she is the fountain head" (G. Glotz : Aegean Civilization, p. 245).

This source of fecundating energy, mother-earth or Prithvi is formulated in many icons which are worshipped and described under various names in Vedic literature, as Aditi, Vinata, Surasa and Sarama.

Terracotta in Bengal

We have already referred to the Indus Valley (C. 2000 B. C.) and the Mayuryan terracottas (C. 300 B. C.) of Bihar. We now come to the phases revealed in the Culture of Bengal.

In Bengal, Terracottas appear in three distinct evolutionary stages. In the primitive stage, it partakes of the character of Mayuryan and Pre-Mayuryan Art of greater India, the nearest culture-area being the old site of Laurya Nandangarh, near Bettiah.

In the year 1929-30, some terracotta figurines of the Sunga Period were found at Mahasthangarh in the Bogra District. These finds help us to confirm the fact that Mahasthan represents one of the earliest of city-sites of Bengal and was in occupation from the 2nd century B. C. to the 12th century A. D. In November 1931, a small fragmentary stone slab, bearing six lines of a Mayuryan inscription in *Bramhi* characters, has been discovered almost on the surface of the earth, which has created considerable interest among scholars in Bengal. In addition to the identification of Mahasthan with the ancient Pundra-Nagara or Pundra-Vardhana, the date of the site has been pushed back to the 4th century B. C., that is, two centuries earlier than that suggested above, on the strength of a terracotta figurine of the Sunga period discovered here during 1930-31—thus relating the early culture of Bengal to the culture of Mayuryan times.

In this early stage, the terracottas consist of stray cult-pieces of small sizes, analogous to the Bulandibagh and Nandangarh finds. (Bettiah, Champaran District).

To the later phase of Mahasthan Art probably belonging to the Gupta era, belongs a remarkable circular plaque, illustrating a *Mithuna*, depicted against the decorative background of lotus-petals. A very interesting find from Mahasthangarh is a terracotta plaque (Plate 3), depicting the 'Dream of Maya Devi' very skilfully patterned against the square panel by placing the bed diagonally across the plaque, thus introducing a new design different from the primitive illustration of the same theme at Bharhut.

In the next stage, we find terracottas in larger sizes and related to architectural structure, as decorations of the facades of temples.

This is very well-illustrated in the *Mithuna* plaque from Mahasthan cited above and also at Paharpur, and much earlier, at Gokul (near Mahasthan in Bogra District). At this site, we have not only several fragments of human and animal figures, but also many terracotta plaques, some bearing architectural and floral patterns revealing the lotus motif, the chequer and the window patterns. Most of these finds are typically 'Gupta' in style. One unique *Vajra*-motif is of special interest. But when we come to Paharpur, we come across a full-fledged application of terracottas to architectural forms.

On the facades of this Chaumukha temple of the Sarvato-bhadra type (of uncertain date not later than the 8th century A.D.) at Paharpur, we have a large series of beautifully designed terracotta plaques of primitive vitality and designed with a fertile imagination which is truly wonderful. In this series of plaques, we have not only lively representations of the early inhabitants of Bengal—Sabaras and hunting types, but also scenes from the *Krishna-lila.*

The profuse architectural applications of terracottas are met with in the third stage, typically illustrated in the famous temple at Badnagar (Murshidabad) and the beautiful temple at Mathurapur (Faridpur District) and the 'sloping roof' temple at Handial (Pabna District). The decoration of the facades of temple, with fashioned and carved bricks and terracottas, now become a widespread fashion in temple architecture in Bengal. This is well-illustrated in the elegant Sridhara Temple (Bankura), the Lakshmi-Janardan Temple at Ilambazar (Birbhum), and the Basudeva Temple at Bansabati (Hooghly) and the Madanmohan Temple (Bankura) with elaborate representations of themes borrowed from the *Puranas*. If we study the details of the facades of these temples, given in enlarged dimensions (Plates 11, 12, 13, 27, 45), we are struck by the largeness of conception, the dramatic vigour, and by the liveliness of most of these pictures depicted on bricks and plaques, which stand for the vividness of wall-paintings and frescoes, the dearth of which is compensated by these 'pictures' on bricks and plaques. We can only make a passing reference to the remarkable finds, recently discovered by the Calcutta University Archæological Mission from Chandraketugarh, from Beda-champa, (an ancient village in 24 Parganas) and from Hariharpur (nine miles from Calcutta). The former site has yielded many finds which include many early types including terracottas of Mayuryan, and perhaps, Pre-Mayuryan affinities. These valuable finds include some examples of Nude Goddesses and Fertility figurines—which recall such pre-historic models as are cited here from Mesopotamian culture.

We have to make a detailed reference to the recent finds recovered by the Calcutta University Mission from an ancient site at Tamralipta (Tamluk, Midnapur). These interesting terracottas reveal that the ancient port of Tamralipta was once also a centre of great cultural activity since the days of the illustrious Mayurya and Sunga emperors of Pataliputra. Apart from a few pre-historic types, most of these terracottas may be dated chronologically, in the different epochs of the long period extending from about the third century A. D. to about the sixth century A. D. A number of Yakshi figures discovered at Tamluk may be confidently assigned to the Sunga period (150 B. C.) on the basis of their stylistic idioms. Several of them may even go back to the Mayurya epoch. The Yakshis of Tamralipta can be easily related to the terracotta Yakshi figurines of other ancient sites such as those of Patna, Kausambi, Mathura and Taxila. The notable characteristics of the Yakshinis of Tamralipta are their graceful expression and sensitive form, which distinguish them from the terracottas of the northern Indian sites. Apart from a group of Yakshini figures, there is a very interesting terracotta rectangular plaque, depicting four figures, very probably illustrating a Jataka theme, closely following the technique of the railing-figures of Bharhut. The plaque is of moulded type, depicting four figures, one elderly lady caressing a pretty girl by touching her cheek ; the girl which is the central figure in the composition points with endearment to an erect male figure at the extreme right-hand corner, carrying something like a broom-stick. Above these three figures is a beautifully shaped turbaned head, who may be possibly an onlooker or a passer-by. Very probably, this four-figure composition illustrates the Bodhisattva Matanga Jataka. A small hole at the top of the plaque for passing a string, suggests that this terracotta 'picture' was hung up on the wall of some private house. The ladies depicted on this plaque wear elaborate coiffures, the *channavira*, or cross-garlands, cinctures and fine skirts. The general stylistic treatment of this plaque is closely related to the stone-reliefs of Bharhut. And in this connection it should be remembered, that, before the glamourous periods of the Mayuryas and the Sungas, Indian Plastic Art went through a continuous period of art-evolution through the medium of clay, wood and ivory, one after another, before plastic art finally emerged in the material of stone. The terracotta finds from Tamluk brought to light by the Calcutta University, represent the earlier stage of the evolution, earlier than the stone-reliefs of Bharhut. Bachhofer has made very significant remarks in emphasizing on the role of the terracottas in the evolution of stone sculpture : "Long before the Mayurya dyansty, there had already existed in India, an art of wood-carving or clay-sculpture which definitely shaped and modelled the well-known figures of the Yakshis and the Yakshinis. The fact that a century later, the artists of Bharhut operated with firmly outlined types of gods points in this direction" (Early Indian Sculpture, Vol. I., p. 12). As has been pointed out by Sri Paresh Chandra Gupta, of the Ashutosh Museum, "Actually, the richly modelled and lively female figure of Didarganj, the elephant figure of Dhauli, the Asokan pillar capitals as well as the so-called Yakshis of Parkham and Patna are pre-supposed (and anticipated) by a lot of ancient terracotta and clay figures recovered from the various ancient Indian sites already referred to. Several Yakshinis discovered at Tamluk, are of moulded type, and their features, particularly the flattened model possibly take them anterior to the Sunga Period. Some of the jewelleries and costumes as found on the terracottas and clay female figurines of Tamluk are exactly similar to those of the Bharhut representations of Yakshis and Yakshinis. The same elaborate coiffures, the circular and triangular ear-rings, the *channaviras* or double garlands, the prescious looking girdles made of beads or medallions as well as the muslin or silken petticoats of transparent quality,—we find again and again on both the examples of Tamralipta and the Bharhut railings."

A terracotta piece found at Tamluk is of outstanding interest, as it represents a miniature gateway almost similar to the famous railing and carved gateway of the Sanchi Stupa. This piece is therefore unique, and it not only establishes a close link between the art and culture of ancient Vanga and Vidisha, but also throws an important light upon the architecture of Bengal in the Sunga period. Particular interest attaches to the series of dolls and toys recovered from Tamluk of which the most interesting is the toy-chariot with the head of a ram. Toys for boys are referred to in some of the Jataka stories. Thus in the Jataka-story (No. 465) we are told: "When prince Vidudhabha was at the age of seven years, having observed how the other princes received presents of toy-elephants and horses and other toys from the family of their mother's fathers, the lad said to his mother, 'Mother, the rest of them get presents from their mothers' family, but no one sends me anything'". The Pali text makes it clear that toy-elephants *(hathi-rupaka)* and horses *(asva-rupaka)* were often given to juveniles as presents *(panna-kara)*. Similarly, a story of the *Katha-sarit-sagara* also relates how a young child named Somaprabha struck a Siddha with a white toy-elephant of clay.

We are tempted to refer here, very summarily, to the great and ancient tradition of clay-sculpture in Bengal. While in other parts of India outside Bengal, the Siva-linga, the Phallus emblem of Siva, is worshipped in stone, crystal, and even in metal effigies, the hoary tradition in Bengal is to worship this effigy of Siva temporarily made out of clay (*parthivam lingam*). And even in modern Bengal, young girls are taught to worship Siva in crude clay-effigies, generally made out of the mud brought from the bed of the river Ganges (*Ganga-mrittika*). The purpose of this worship of the mud-effigy of Siva is to secure for the child-worshipper a worthy husband equal in virtues to the magnanimous God Siva.

How the great God Siva came to be transferred to the form of a Lingam by the curse of the Sage Bhrigu (*yoni-linga svarupam vai rupam tasmad bhavisyati*) is referred to in an ancient *purana* quoted in the *Sabda-kalpa-druma*, Volume VI, p. 3981-82.

This hoary ancient tradition of fashioning clay images is still honoured to-day in Bengal, with reference to the periodical cult-worship of Durga, Kali, Jagaddhatri, Sarasvati, Kartikeya, Visva Karma, and other minor gods, solemnly observed with elaborate rituals and festivities. The clay-images of Bengal offer a shining gallery of gods and goddesses, which deserve a separate monograph, and we can only be satisfied here, by this summary allusion to a great tradition.

Thus the terracottas of Bengal provide a unique and brilliant chapter in the history of Bengali Art throughout the centuries, in a series of progressive chronological sequences.

PLATES

Plate 1. Terracotta Female figurine (Mother-Goddess), Circa 3rd Millennium B.C., Harappa, West Panjab.

Plate 2. Terracotta Female figurine, Circa, 3rd Millennium B.C., Mohenja-Daro, Sind.

Plate 3. Terracotta plaque, Mayadevi's dream, Mahasthan, Dist. Bogra, East Bengal.

Plate 4. Terracotta plaque, Buffalo in repose, Mainamati, Dist. Comilla, East Bengal.

Plate 5. Terracotta medallion, Mithuna, Mahasthan, Dist. Bogra, East Bengal.

Plate 6. Terracotta plaque, Old man returning home, Paharpur, Dist. Bogra, East Bengal.

Plate 7. Terracotta plaque, Huntress carrying prey, Paharpur, Dist. Bogra, East Bengal.

Plate 8. Terracotta plaque, scenes from Krishna's life, Paharpur, Dist. Bogra, East Bengal.

Plate 9. General view of Jorbangla Temple, Dist. Nadia, West Bengal.

Plate 10. General view of Palpara Temple, Palpara, Near Chakdah, Dist. Nadia, West Bengal.

Plate 11. Front view of Sridhar Temple, Dist. Bankura, West Bengal.

Plate 12. Facade of Sridhar Temple showing Terracotta work, Dist. Bankura, West Bengal.

Plate 13. Facade of Lakshmi-Janardan Temple showing Terracotta work, Ilambazar, Dist. Birbhum, West Bengal.

Plate 14. Terracotta panels depicting Saiva legends, Sridhar Temple, Dist. Bankura, West Bengal.

Plate 15. Terracotta panels showing scenes from Krishna's life, Lakshmi-Janardan Temple, Ilambazar, Dist. Birbhum, West Bengal.

Plate 16. Terracotta panels showing scenes from the Ramayana, Lakshmi-Janardan Temple, Ilambazar, Dist. Birbhum, West Bengal.

Plate 17. Durga (Mahisasuramardini), Lakshmi-Janardan Temple, Ilambazar, Dist. Birbhum, West Bengal.

Plate 18. Terracotta panels showing scenes from Krishna's life, Charbangla Temple (North), Baranagar, Dist. Murshidabad, West Bengal.

Plate 19. Terracotta panels depicting Balalila episodes of Krishna's life, Kali Temple, Baranagar, Dist. Murshidabad, West Bengal.

Plate 20. Wall frieze with decorative motifs, Sridhar Temple, Dist. Bankura, West Bengal.

Plate 21. Section of an ornamented pillar, Kali Temple, Baranagar, Dist. Murshidabad, West Bengal.

Plate 22. Section of an ornamented pillar, Kali Temple, Baranagar, Dist, Murshidabad, West Bengal.

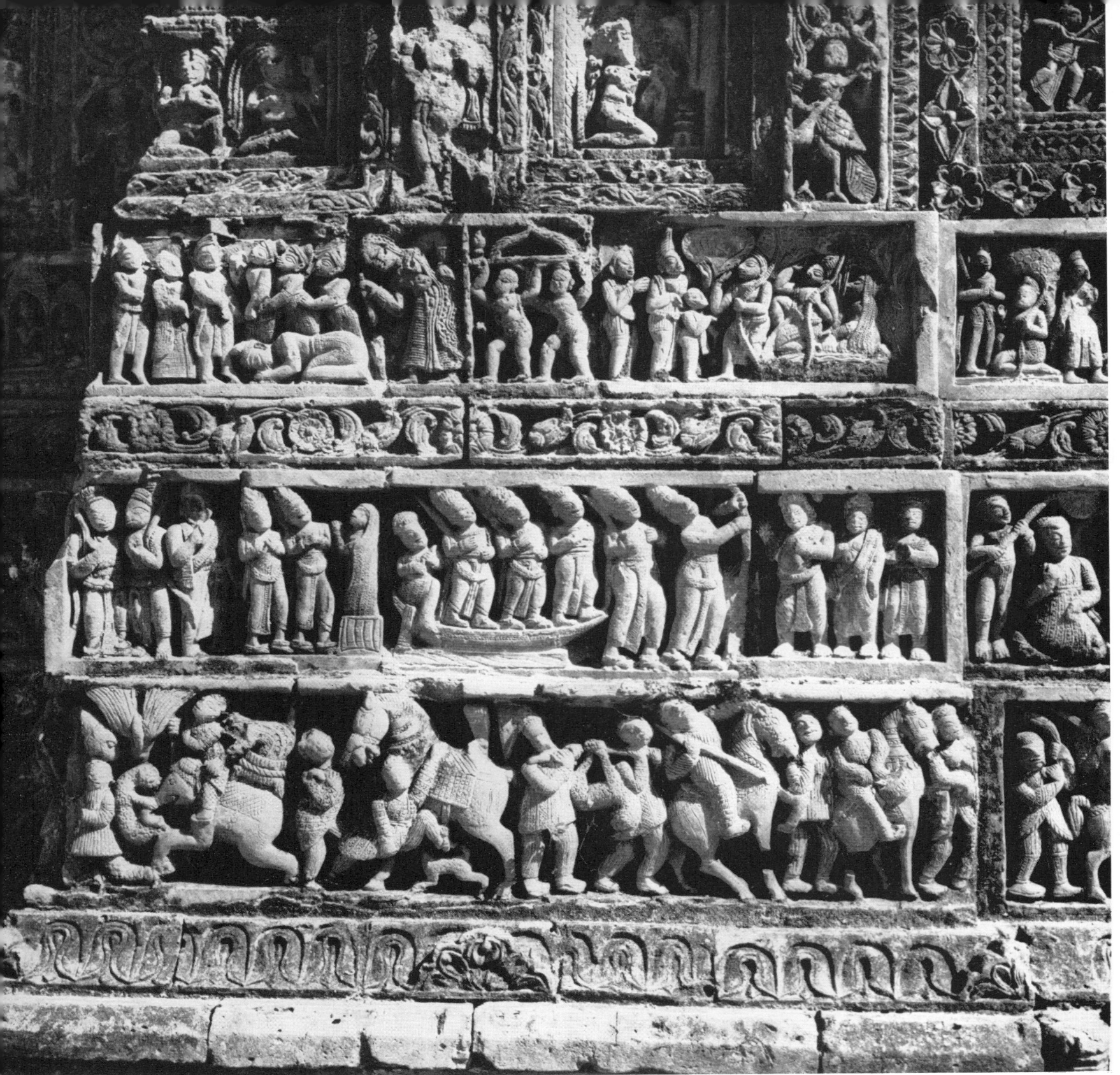

Plate. 23. Terracotta panels showing scenes from the Ramayana, Kali Temple, Baranagar, Dist. Murshidabad, West Bengal.

Plate 24. Terracotta panels showing scenes from Krishna's life, Kali Temple, Baranagar, Dist. Murshidabad, West Bengal.

Plate 25. Terracotta panels depicting scenes from Krishna's life, Kali Temple, Dist. Murshidabad, West Bengal.

Plate 26. Terracotta panels showing scenes from the Ramayana, Kamarpara Temple, Dist. Hooghly, West Bengal.

Plate 27. Wall frieze with different decorative motifs and Terracotta panels, Basudeva Temple, Bansabati, Dist. Hooghly, West Bengal.

Plate 28. Ornamented pillar, Sridhar Temple, Bishnupur, Dist. Bankura, West Bengal.

Plate 29. Ornamented Terracotta panels on the wall, Birnagar Temple, Dist. Nadia, West Bengal.

Plate 30. Terracotta panels depicting scenes from the Ramayana, Charbangla Temple (North) Baranagar, Dist. Murshidabad, West Bengal.

Plate 31. Terracotta panels showing scenes from Krishna's life, Basudeva Temple, Bansabati, Dist. Hooghly, West Bengal.

Plate 32. Section (lower portion) of an ornamented pillar, Basudeva Temple, Bansabati, Dist. Hooghly, West Bengal.

Plate 33. Terracotta relief, scenes from the Ramayana, Charbangla Temple (East), Baranagar, Dist. Murshidabad, West Bengal.

Plate 34. Goddess Kali, Charbangla Temple (North), Baranagar, Dist. Murshidabad, West Bengal.

Plate 35. Female followers of Chandi fighting the demons, Charbangla Temple (West), Baranagar, Dist. Murshidabad, West Bengal.

Plate 36. Goddess Chandi, fighting the demons, Charbangla Temple (West), Baranagar, Dist. Murshidabad, West Bengal.

Plate 37. Scenes from the Ramayana (battle between Rama and Ravana), Charbangla Temple (North), Baranagar, Dist. Murshidabad, West Bengal.

Plate 38. Goddess Sakti (Kali) slaying the demon, Charbangla Temple (North), Baranagar, Dist. Murshidabad, West Bengal.

Plate 39. Krishna slaying Kuvalayapida, Charbangla Temple (North), Baranagar, Dist. Murshidabad, West Bengal.

Plate 40. Krishna slaying Kansa, Charbangla Temple (North), Baranagar, Dist. Murshidabad, West Bengal.

Plate 41. Ganga, Charbangla Temple, (North), Baranagar, Dist. Murshidabad, West Bengal.

Plate 42. Gaja-Lakshmi, Charbangla Temple (North), Baranagar, Dist. Murshidabad, West Bengal.

Plate 43.   Mahisasuramardini, Charbangla Temple (North), Baranagar, Dist. Murshidabad, West Bengal.

Plate 44. Annapurna giving alms to Shiva, Charbangla Temple (South), Dist. Murshidabad, West Bengal.

Plate 45. Krishna dancing with followers, Madanmohan Temple, Bishnupur, Dist. Bankura, West Bengal.

Plate 46. Terracotta panels depicting the battle between Rama and Ravana, Jaydev Temple, Jaydev Kenduli, Dist. Birbhum, West Bengal.

Plate 47. Terracotta panels showing scenes from the Ramayana, Surul Temple, Surul, Dist. Birbhum, West Bengal.

Plate 48. Terracotta panels depicting battle scenes from the Ramayana, Sural Temple, Sural, Dist. Birbhum, West Bengal.

Plate 49. Terracotta panels showing scenes from the Ramayana, Surul Temple, Surul, Dist. Birbhum, West Bengal.

Plate 50. Terracotta panels depicting scenes from the Ramayana, entrance of Palpara Temple, Chakdah, Dist. Nadia, West Bengal.

Notes on the Plates

PLATE 1 : Terracotta female figurine (Mother-Goddess), circa 3rd Millennium B.C., Harappa, West Punjab. Primitive in appearance and in technique, this terracotta figurine from Harappa represents a standing female, nude but for a short loin-cloth, and adorned with a neck-collar and an elaborate fan-shaped head-dress with a shell-like pannier on each side. Modelled in the round entirely by the hand, its features and adornments—viz., eyes, lips, breasts, head-dress, neck-collar and loin-cloth—are fashioned separately from pellets or strips of clay and then applied to the modelled form by the applique technique. The nature and purpose of this and similar female figurines found from the Harappa culture-sites are obscure, though the generality of scholarly opinion is inclined to regard them as a "manifestation of the great Mother Goddess." Crude in features, but carefully modelled with all the details of anatomy (the legs and hands are, however, broken in this specimen) and decoration, it "suggests a greater freedom of movements indicating a stylistic advance on the figurines of the peasant (Kulli and Zhob) cultures, though the religious association of both appears to be the same."

PLATE 2 : Terracotta female figurine, circa 3rd Millennium B.C., Mohenjo-daro, Sind. This is another female figurine, representing the Mother-goddess (?) from the sister city of Mohenjo-daro, similarly made, dressed and adorned as that from Harappa (cf. Plate 1). The pinched up nose and the applied lips and eyes give a goat-like expression to the countenance.

PLATE 3 : This is a remarkable terracotta plaque, depicting the old Buddhist legend of the "Dream of Maya Devi" before her conception. The lady is represented as lying on a bedstead with decorated legs. The artist has given a new treatment of the scene by placing the bedstead (*palanka*) diagonally against the square panel. The empty spaces below the bed are filled by some domestic furniture—spittoons, lamp-stands (?) etc. These are balanced by the flowering end of the lady's *sari* at the top, which suggests the agitation of the lady when in her dream the birth of the Buddha was announced.

PLATE 4 : It is a remarkable study of a recumbent buffalo, scratching its ears by its leg, depicted on a terracotta plaque from Mainamati (ancient Pattikhera in Tippera). Mainamati (recently excavated by the Archaeological Department) has yielded various archaeological remains—terracottas, carved bricks and cult images associated with the Buddhist Cults and of the later cults of the Nathas—popularized by King Gopichandra and his queen Madanavati (Mainamati). A similar motif, of a bull scratching its mouth will be found on a terracotta plaque, dug up from Salban Raja Palace Mount at Mainamati (see Pl. VII, Archaeological Activities in Pakistan, Annual Bibliography of Indian Archaeology, 1948-53). Stylistically, this piece of plaque has close semblance to the terracotta plaques of Paharpur.

PLATE 5 : In this circular medallion from Mahasthan (Bogra District) we have the representation of a *Mithuna*, a reproductive couple, which has been used as an auspicious masonic symbol, placed on temples of all Schools of Indian Architecture—Buddhist, Bramhanical and Jaina. The significance of this sexual symbol has been discussed in an article published in *Rupam* (No. 22-23, April-July, 1925, p. 54). Mahasthan has been identified with the site of the ancient city of Pundra-Vardhana, the antiquity of which goes back to the time of the Mayuryyas. The site has yielded various archaeological remains, dating from the third century B. C. to the time of the Palas (8th century A. D.). The *Mithuna* plaque can be dated in the Gupta period on the basis of the dwarfish types and style of the two human figures depicted on the medallion.

PLATE 6 : A terracotta plaque from Paharpur, depicting a running old man with a beard, carrying on his shoulder something which looks like carcasses of animals which have been killed by the instrument held in the right hand. The old man is naked, except for a piece of rope tied round his waist. He is probably a man of the hunting tribe of Sabaras, a non-Aryan tribe, at one time inhabiting in Bengal, but now surviving in Orissa.

PLATE 7 : Another terracotta plaque from Paharpur. It depicts a woman of the Sabara tribe, who used to live by hunting. In contemporary literature, we have many refluences to this primitive non-Aryan tribe, some of whom wore no clothes, and some of whom wore leaves of trees to cover their nakedness. This class was designated by the term, *parna-sabari*, as illustrated in the type depicted here. She is carrying in her left hand an animal, probably a jackal which she has killed. The Sabaras possessed a culture of their own. The cult of Jagannatha is said to have come from the Sabaras or Saoras, who are still associated with some rituals observed in the worship of Jagannatha at Puri. The non-Aryan melody Saveri (Saverika) is a gift of the Sabaras to Indian Music.

PLATE 8 : A rectangular terracotta plaque from Paharpur, depicting a scene from Krishna's life.

PLATE 9 : General view of Jorbangla Temple, Dist. Nadia, West Bengal. Built entirely of brick, this perfect specimen of the Jorbangla temples of Bengal is, in fact, a 'twin temple' resembling two bungalow-cottages joined together. The name of these temples has been derived from their peculiar triangular double-roofs, the ends of which look like a big M. The simplest variety, of which this is an example, has only spires represented by one or more (here, three) iron spikes on each roof. Originating from the thatch and bamboo cottages (*dochalas*) of Bengal, with curved eaves and roofs having two sloping sides ending in a ridge, these temples may be "defined as an indigenous form of building art particularly expressive of the inhabitants of Bengal."

PLATE 10 : General view of Palpara Temple, Palpara, near Chakdah, Dist. Nadia, West Bengal. A general view of the brick-built Palpara Temple, a perfect specimen of the simplest variety of the Bengal hut-type temples, the roofs of which are fashioned after the ordinary *chauchala* huts of Bengal. Designed as a structure, square in plan, this temple has tall vertical walls, the lines and planes of which are carried across its facade in a series of parallel bow-like curves, surmounted by triangular coverings, curved like the segment of a circle at its base, on four sides of the roof, converging at the point of the apex like a curvilinear pyramid, and having only one spire at the top. With curved contour and consequent stunted height, the importance of this and similar temples lies mainly "as a reflection of racial characteristics."

PLATE 11 : Front view of the Sridhara Temple, Dist. Bankura, West Bengal. A further development on the ordinary *chauchala* temples is marked by the substitution of spired towers, of which this *panchavimsa-ratna* temple, having twenty-four towers running up the sides of its domical roof in two tiers crowned by a large tower at the centre, is a specimen. The upper portion of these towers are fashioned into a kind of *sikharas* with horizontal courses of mouldings. Lacking in the stately grandeur of the *sikharas* of Orissan temples, the main attraction of this temple lies in its ornamented facade consisting of three arched openings between two substantial pillars, and decorated externally with terracotta panels of relief work over its entire surface, which imparts to it a peculiar lyric beauty and freshness that makes sensuous appeal to the eyes of the spectator.

PLATE 12 : Facade of the Sridhara Temple, Dist. Bankura, West Bengal, showing terracotta work. This is a view of the front facade of the temple, every inch of which, beginning from below the eaves down to the very level of the plinth, is richly decorated with terracotta plaques. The most important panels are the three just above the arched doorways of the temple. These are large story-telling panels depicting scenes from the Saiva and Vaishnava legends. Besides, there are horizontal and vertical rows of plaques showing sundry deities of the Hindu pantheon, *Mithunas* and other figures. On either side of the facade, is a continuous vertical row of 'lion and horse-rider' motifs. The decoration also consists of rosettes, ornamental patterns and scroll work.

PLATE 13: Facade of Lakshmi-Janardana Temple, Ilambazar, Dist. Birbhum, West Bengal, showing terracotta work. Besides scroll work and floral motifs, the decorations of this ornamented facade consists of three large panels, just above the arched doorways of the temple,—one of them showing scenes from the early exploits of Krishna as given in the Vaishnava texts; another, those of Rama as given in the Ramayana of Krittivasa; and the third a representation of Sakti in one of her most well-known forms. Another continuous horizontal panel runs along the entire breadth of the facade. Rows of terracotta plaques, some of which contains representations of a purely domestic and secular character, are seen on the borders of the doorway.

PLATE 14: Terracotta panels depicting Saiva legends, Sridhara Temple, Bishnupur, Dist. Bankura, West Bengal. These two panels occupy the space above the left-hand doorway of the temple. The lower panel depicts the marriage of Siva and Parvati (Kalyanasundara-murti). This is a story-telling panel, comparable in its magnitude, though in a small compass, to the famous portrayal of the same theme on the walls of the Elephanta Cave (cf. Art of the Rashtrakutas, Plate 40) and not an image stele like that of the Dacca Museum specimen from Rampal (cf. Bhattasali, Iconography of the Buddhist and Brahmanic Sculptures in the Dacca Museum, Plate XLVII, b). The stage of the scene is the marriage-pandal, decorated with curtains, seen above the heads of the people on the right. In the centre of the scene stands Siva, the bridegroom, profusely decorated with ornaments, wearing *jatamukuta* on the head and a garland of snakes round the neck, but naked. The bride, Parvati, is seen on the right, seated on a wooden stool, borne by two men to be carried by them round the bridegroom (*pradakshina*) seven times, as is required by Bengali marriage custom. In front of them, are seated two priests, one of them reading from a manuscript. On the extreme right of the scene is a female blowing by the mouth (*huludhvani*). On the extreme left, stands the three-faced Brahma, next to him is Vishnu (?) and then comes Himalaya, the bride's father, with an attendant. The way in which the marriage scene has been depicted has something peculiarly familiar to Bengal about it. The scene does not appear to have taken place in distant Himalaya, "but in the artists' own home-surroundings among the villages of Bengal with Bengali men and women as their heroes and heroines". The upper panel possibly depicts the birth-rites (*jatakarma*) of Kartikeya, the son of Siva and Parvati. The dramatis personae in both the panels are clad in garments as were worn by high-class Bengali gentlemen of about the 18th century A. D.

PLATE 15: Terracotta panels showing scenes from Krishna's life, Lakshmi-Janardana Temple, Ilambazar, Dist. Birbhum, West Bengal. These panels, showing scenes from the early life (*bala-lila*) of Krishna, occupy part of the space above the central doorway of the temple. The lowermost panel shows the boy Krishna accompanied by Baladeva and the other cow-boys (*gopa-valakas*), about to depart from his foster-mother's house towords the grazing grounds (*goshtha*) for tending the cattle. Yasoda, the foster-mother, is seen exhorting Baladeva and others to look after the boy Krishna while away at the fields. In the middle panel, are shown Krishna and Baladeva, together with all their juvenile companions, making mirth and frolic at the ranches in the intervals of attending to the cows. The uppermost panel shows Krishna suppressing the serpent king Kaliya (*Kaliya-damana*), who lived in the depths of the Yamuna near to the grazing grounds and used to poison the air and waters of the neighbourhood with fatal effect upon the cow-boys and the cattle. The boy godhead suppressed him with his enormous might and then mounting on his cluster of heads began to dance. He pardoned the

Naga only when his wives implored him to save them from widowhood by sparing their husband. The solitary Kadamba tree, once the perching place of Garuda, which escaped the effects of the Naga's venom, is shown on the left of the scene. The roundel on the upper left corner depicts the *Rasa-lila* episode. Krishna with Radha on his left, is standing in the *vidgala* attitude in the centre of the Rasachakra; around them dance the Gopinis, and the hero, multiplying himself into many Krishnas, dance between each pair of maidens in a ring.

PLATE 16 : Terracotta panels showing scenes from Ramayana, Lakshmi-Janardana Temple, Ilambazar, Dist. Birbhum, West Bengal. These panels occupy the space above the left-hand doorway of the temple. The lowermost panel, just above the cusped arch of the doorway, depicts the epic battle of Rama against Ravana. Both the adversaries are standing on chariots drawn by horses. Rama's chariot has a curvilinear *sikhara* of the Rekha *deuls* with horizontal bands running around it, while that of Ravana is surmounted by a stepped pyramidal *sikhara* of the Bhadra *deul* type. The uppermost panel shows Rama enthroned with his wife in open *darbar* after his return from Lanka, attended by his half-brothers, Bharata (holding the parasol), Satrughna (waving a palm-leaf fan) and Lakshmana (serving as the *dvarapala*) and also by his simian councillors Hanumana and Jambuvana and others. On the extreme left, is seen a *vaitalika* playing on drums. The middle panel perhaps depicts the performance of the *Asvamedha* sacrifice by Rama.

PLATE 17 : Durga (Mahishasura-mardini), Lakshmi-Janardana Temple, Ilambazar, Dist. Birbhum, West Bengal. These panles, just above the right-hand doorway of the temple, show the ten-armed Durga killing the Buffalo-demon (Mahishasura), accompanied by all the members of her family (*saparivara*), the form in which she is worshipped at the autumnal festival of Bengal in the present day. This presentation of the goddess is not a covering image (*avarana-devata*), usually found on the walls of temples, but a story-telling scene depicting the performance of a Durga-Puja festival in Bengal.

PLATE 18 : Terracotta panels showing scenes from Krishna's life, Charbangla Temple (North), Baranagar, Dist. Murshidabad, West Bengal. The upper panel depicts the charming *Dana-lila* episode of Krishna's early life, representing milk-maids carrying pots of milk and curd on their heads and Krishna, seated under a tree, accompanied by his playmates realising the lover's toll from them. The lyrical beauty of this scene attracts notice. The lower panel is secular in theme; it shows a gentleman riding on an open phaeton drawn by two caparisoned horses and attended by two sentinels (*paiks*) carrying guns.

PLATE 19 : Terracotta panels depicting *Bala-lila* episodes of Krishna's life, Kali Temple, Baranagar, Dist. Murshidabad, West Bengal. Lower centre—Krishna and Baladeva stealing butter, while their foster-mother, Yasoda, is engaged in churning milk. Lower left—Yasoda milking the cow (only part of the scene is visible). Lower right—Child Krishna breaking the twin Arjuna trees. Upper centre—the *Vastra-harana* (stealing the garments) episode. Upper left—Krishna killing the demon Kesin.

PLATE 20 : Wall-frieze with different decorative motifs, Sridhara Temple, Dist. Bankura, West Bengal. This is a detailed view of a part of the wall, ornamented with various decorative motifs, adjacent to the left-hand doorway of the temple. The decoration consists of vertical bands of floral designs, mainly meandering lotus creepers; another vertical band (on the left), consisting of a succession of super-imposed *sardula* motifs, and a series of vertically arranged terracotta plaques (on the right) containing *mithunas* in various attitudes. The *sardula* or *gajavyala* representing a lion, rampant on an elephant, is a very old decorative motif in Indian art. From this idea, the Bengali sculptor has created a conventional *sardula*, jumping upon a rider on horseback, who has been sandwiched between his mount below and the mythical feline above. The Bengali sculptor has thus made an original contribution even while borrowing the idea from preceding tradition.

PLATE 21 : Section of an ornamented pillar, Kali Temple, Baranagar, Dist. Murshidabad, West Bengal. The ornamentation consists of horizontal bands of rosettes, lotus-petal designs and scroll motifs and a series of terracotta panels containing figure sculptures inside niches, possibly depicting episodes from the *Bala-lila* of Krishna.

PLATE 22 : Section of an ornamented pillar, Kali Temple, Baranagar, Dist. Murshidabad, West Bengal. This is a section of another pillar, ornamented in a similar fashion as the preceding one. The central panel depicts the *Vastra-harana* episode of the Krishna-lila. The frolicsome hero, playing on his pipe, is seen seated high on a tree, from the branches of which are hanging the clothes of the *gopinis*, stolen by him while they were bathing in the Yamuna. The embarrassed women-folk, concealing their modesty by placing the palms of their hands on the pubes or by sitting on the haunches with the knees drawn close together, are seen entreating the boy to return their garments. The panel on the right shows an image of Vishnu riding on Garuda. The iconography and plastic modelling of this image follow the sculptural traditions of the Pala period.

PLATE 23 : Terracotta panel depicting scenes from the Ramayana, Kali Temple, Baranagar, Dist. Murshidabad, West Bengal. The lowermost panel, just above the plinth, depicts a tiger-hunt. The sympathetic as well as naturalistic portrayal of animal and human life in this scene deserves notice. The spirited movement of the attacking elephant, the last struggle for life by the exasperated victim of the hunt, the bewildered amazement of the frightened *mahut*, the agility of movement of the cavalier about to mount his steed by placing one of his feet on the stirrup, and the triumphant exit of the party after the successful conclusion of the hunt—all these have been very truthfully portrayed by the unknown artist. The next two panels depict scenes from the Ramayana. The middle panel deals with the incidents prior to Rama's marriage with Sita, viz., (from left to right) (1) Rama and Lakshmana, accompanied by Visvamitra, on their way to Mithila. (2) Rama releasing Ahalya from the lithic form, which she had assumed owing to a curse by her husband Gautama ; (3) Rama, Lakshmana and Visvamitra crossing the Saraju river by boat on their way to Mithila ; (4) Rama breaking the Hara-dhanu (Bow of Siva) as a preliminary to wooing Sita. The uppermost panel is concerned with some episodes of Rama's exile, viz., (from left to right) (1) Rama's meeting with Bharata (Bharata-milana), who came to the forest to dissuade the former from going into exile ; (2) Rama, Lakshmana and Sita in the Panchavati forest, receiving homage from a Rishi family (?).

PLATE 24 : Terracotta panels depicting scenes from Krishna's life, Kali Temple, Baranagar, Dist. Murshidabad, West Bengal. The lowermost panel portrays a deer-hunt by a group of men, some of whom are on foot, some on horse-back and others on the *howdah*. The next two panels depict scenes from the life of Krishna. The second panel from below concerns itself with the incidents relating to the birth of Krishna. On the right is shown the prison in which Kangsa had confined the parents of his future chastiser, where, on that eventful midnight of the eighth *tithi* of the dark half of Bhadrapada when the Lord was born in this earth, all the sentinels appointed by Kangsa fell fast asleep ; and on the threshold of the prison is shown the mother handing over the new-born babe to the father to be safely transported to Yasoda, the wife of Nanda, at Gokul on the other side of the Yamuna. On the extreme left is shown Vasudeva crossing the Yamuna with the babe in his arms.

PLATE 25 : Terracotta panels depicting scenes from Krishna's life, Kali Temple, Baranagar, Dist. Murshidabad, West Bengal. The upper panel depicts the birth and transportation of Krishna to Yasoda's house. The lower panel is the representation of an aristocratic journey of the 18th century showing a lady riding on a *palki*, borne by a group of four bearers and a gentleman riding on a carriage, drawn by horses. A group of horsemen and elephant riders as well as two sentinels carrying guns accompany the nobleman and his lady as escorts.

PLATE 26 : Terracotta panels showing scenes from the Ramayana, Kamarpara Temple, Dist. Hooghly, West Bengal. The two panels in the middle show Siva riding on his bull, attended by a monkey in front and a Gana behind (right) ; and Durga Mahishasura-mardini, accompanied by his sons and daughters (left). Above and below are the monkey hosts of Rama fighting against Ravana and his Rakshasa legions.

PLATE 27 : Wall-frieze with different decorative motifs and terracotta panels, Basudeva Temple, Bansabati, Dist. Hooghly, West Bengal. The decoration consists of lotus-medallions, rosettes, floral and foliage designs and scroll motifs. In the centre there is a roundel containing a representation of the *Rasa-lila* episode. In a panel at the bottom is shown the *Putana-vadha* episode (i.e. Krishna killing the ogress *Putana* who was engaged by Kangsa to destroy the child Krishna). The small medallion within this panel depicts the slaying of Kangsa by Krishna.

PLATE 28 : Lower portion of an ornamented pillar, Sridhara Temple, Bishnupur, Dist. Bankura, West Bengal. The ornamentation consists of horizontal bands of rosettes, foliage designs and scroll work and a series of terracotta plaques, the topmost row of which contains each a female figure standing under an arched niche carrying a pitcher by the left arm. The middle row of plaques shows each a male figure standing under a flowery bower ; while the row at the bottom contains a series of human heads.

PLATE 29 : Wall-frieze ornamented with terracotta panels, Birnagar Temple, Dist. Nadia, West Bengal. At the top is Durga Mahishasura-mardini, accompanied by his sons and daughters (*saparivara*). At the bottom is shown the voyage of a sea-going vessel manned by a number of oarsmen and a boatman. At the prow of the ship there is a cabin inside which is seated a passenger. All the sailors as well as the passengers are dressed like Abyssinian Habsis. This scene perhaps depicts the voyage of a vessel the Mughal nauara. In the middle there is a long panel showing a row of swans in various attitudes. At the right end of this panel is a man fighting with a lion. The naturalistic portrayal of the swans and the great vigour displayed by the fighting man and lion evoke from us warm admiration ; the depiction of sailors and passengers of the boat has a peculiarity and charm of its own.

PLATE 30 : Terracotta panels depicting scene from the Ramayana, Charbangla Temple (North), Baranagar, Dist. Murshidabad, West Bengal. The upper panel depicts the performance of the *Putreshthi* sacrifice by Rishyasringa, the deer-headed sage, for Dasaratha, as a preliminary to the birth of Rama and his three half-brothers. The deer-headed sage is seen throwing oblations into the sacrificial fire by a sacrificial laddle, in front of him is standing Dasaratha with his three queens, Kausalya, Kaikayee and Sumitra. The lower panel is a depiction of a contemporary aristocratic journey showing a lady being borne by a group of palanquin-bearers, and accompanied by an escort of horsemen and an elephant rider who is shooting at a tiger from his *howdah*—an indication of the perils of a journey in those days. On the extreme right is shown a man slaying a lion. The stylised presentation of the lion with its elongated face and schematic mane should be noted.

PLATE 31 : Terracotta panels showing scenes from Krishna's life, Basudeva Temple, Bansabati, Dist. Hooghly, West Bengal. The upper panel depicts episodes from the *Bala-lila* of Krishna. The scenes on the right side of the panel cannot be properly identified ; those on the left are as follows ; (1) Krishna stealing butter while Yasoda is engaged in churning milk ; (2) Krishna breaking the twin Arjuna trees, the two released Yakshas are seen standing in front of the crawling child with folded hands. The lower panel shows a man riding on a *palki* borne by a group of palanquin-bearers and a group of ladies riding on a carriage drawn by a pair of bullocks. This scene, no doubt, depicts an aristocratic journey of the 18th century. The peculiar head-dress of the palanquin-bearers and attendants draws notice. They have long *feeringi* caps on their heads.

PLATE 32 : Section (lower portion) of an ornamented pillar, Basudeva Temple, Bansabati, Dist. Hooghly, West Bengal. The ornamentation consists of floral motifs and arabesque work. At the bottom, there is a row of terracotta plaques showing deities from the Brahmanic pantheon, as follows : (from the left to the right) Four-faced Brahma on *hamsa* ; Siva and Parvati (Uma-Mahesvara) on the bull; Durga (Mahishasura-mardini) with her sons and daughters; Vishnu riding on Garuda. The great vigour displayed by the fighting goddess and the demon imparts a majesty dignity to plastic modelling of the Mahishasura-mardini group.

PLATE 33 : Scenes from the Ramayana, Charbangla Temple (East), Baranagar, Dist. Murshidabad, West Bengal. These sculptures, depicting stories from Rama's life, are modelled in relief on clay surface, just above the doorway of the temple. The following scenes can be identified. (1) Rama, accompanied by Sita and Lakshmana, is returning to Ayodhya on Ravana's *vimana* (airship) after the expiry of his fourteen years' of exile. (2) Rama enthroned in open *darbar*, attended by Sita, Lakshmana, Bharata, Hanumana and Jambuvana. (3) Rama and Lakshmana performing the *Asvamedha* sacrifice.

PLATE 34 : Goddess Kali, Charbangla Temple (North), Baranagar, Dist Murshidabad, West Bengal. This presentation of the four-armed figure of Kali is one of the *avarana-devatas*, occupying the facades of the temple. Her iconographic features—trampling over the prostrate body of her husband, carrying the *khadga* and a severed human head, wearing a garland of human skulls (*munda-mala*), attended by a *dakini* and a jackal drinking the blood trickling from the severed human head held in one of her arms—are the same as those of the image which are worshipped under the same name in modern times. The elaborate scroll and floral border around the image deserve notice. The elaborate design and minute execution of the different motifs, particularly of the lotus-creeper and flowers, some of which have stylised birds perching on them and pecking the petals, are very effective and claim high appreciation.

PLATE 35 : Female followers of Chandi fighting the demons, Charbangla Temple (West), Baranagar, Dist. Murshidabad, West Bengal. Sword in hand, these female spirits (*dakinis*) of Chandi have been depicted as if flying in the air in great force and rapidity. Though completely naked they wear ornaments on their persons, particularly a jewelled *mekhala* round the waist and a *channavira* passing over the shoulders and below the sides. It should be noted that these two items of jewellery are very intimately connected with the fertility goddesses, viz., the Yakshinis and Vrikshakas, of early times. The sensuous delineation of the soft anatomy of the body, the gliding contour of the plump and rounded limbs with no breakage in the sinuous curve of the line indicating great action and movement bespeak of a high order of modelling as illustrated in the depiction of these female figures.

PLATE 36 : Goddess Chandi fighting the demons, Charbangla Temple (West), Baranagar, Dist. Murshidabad, West Bengal. This terracotta panel depicts one of the innumerable struggles which the goddess Sakti waged against the demondom. With a coat of chain-mail covering her body from neck to foot and mounted on a fully caparisoned steed which is on full gallop, she is charging her adversaries in hot haste with sword and shield in her hands. The mangled corpse of a decapitated victim is seen lying below, on whose severed head a vultere is feasting. The foliage decorations on the right showing blossoming twigs (*kisalaya*) deserve notice for their elaborate design and minute execution.

PLATE 37 : Scene from the Ramayana (the battle between Rama and Ravana), Charbangla Temple (North), Baranagar, Dist. Murshidabad, West Bengal. This panel, just above the central doorway of the temple, depicts with a marked degree of dash and vigour, the epic battle between Rama and Ravana. Ravana is seen standing on his car, represented by a platform on four wheels drawn by horses, in an attitude of resignation, with his natural hands folded in adoration of his irresistible adversaries Rama and Lakshmana, who are being borne in triumph on the shoulders of their simian supporters and are seen shooting volleys of arrows at their ten-headed and twenty-armed opponent. The scene depicts the last stages of the final struggle when Ravana was on the point of being overpowered.

PLATE 38 : Goddess Sakti slaying demons, Charbangla Temple (North), Baranagar, Dist. Murshidabad, West Bengal. This panel occupying part of the space just above the left-hand doorway of the temple, depicts Sakti (Chandi) fighting against the demons (*asuras*). Springing on her lion mount in great force, the four-handed goddess has caught hold by one of her left hands, of the demon's crown of hair who is seen defending himself with sword and shield standing straight on the *howdah*, and is about to deal the mortal blow at him by her carved sword (*khadga*) held in one of her hands. This is a remarkably dramatic presentation of Sakti's innumerable struggles against the demondom. The lolling tongue and portruding eyes impart a fierce, almost diabolic, aspect to her face ; and the sinuous carve of her body is a gesture of her latent vigour and forceful movement.

PLATE 39 : Krishna slaying Kuvalayapida, Charbangla Temple (North), Baranagar, Dist. Murshidabad, West Bengal. This panel, occupying part of the space above the arch of the right-hand doorway, shows Krishna slaying the elephant Kuvalayapida, who was engaged by Kangsa to kill his future chastiser. On the right, the juvenile hero is seen grappling with the mighty elephant by seizing his tusks. Kuvalayapida is in reality a *danava* who has assumed the form of an elephant ; and on the left of the panel he has reassumed his original demoniac appearance and is on the point of succumbing at the blows of his opponent.

PLATE 40 : Krishna slaying Kangsa, Charbangla Temple (North), Baranagar, Dist. Murshidabad, West Bengal. This panel, above the right-hand doorway of the temple, shows Krishna, followed by Baladeva, slaying Kangsa, the tyrant king of Mathura. Seated in full regalia on his throne under the royal parasol, and girt with a dagger, sword and shield the tyrant is being seen trampled by the right foot of his adolescent adversary, who has caught hold of the crown of his head from which the royal diadem has toppled to the ground and is about to impart a deadly blow by the fist of his right hand.

PLATE 41 : Ganga, Charbangla Temple (North), Baranagar, Dist. Murshidabad, West Bengal. This representation of the goddess Ganga is on a triangular terracotta corner-plaque at one of the extremities of the Northern facade of the temple, just below the carved eaves of the roof. In ancient Indian temples, the river goddesses Ganga and Yamuna are found depicted on jambs on either side of the doorway, generally standing in the *vidgala* attitude, Ganga on her mount the snouted crocodile Makara and Yamuna on the tortoise. Here the exigencies of space have made the artist represent the deity to recline on the back of her mount, a posture quite unconventional. The profuse decorations on her person, the turretted *ardhamukuta*, the flowing garland, and other items of jewellery—all elaborately designed and rhythmically disposed—emphasize the smooth beauty of the exquisitely modelled anatomy of the exposed regions of her figure, viz., the graceful sensitiveness of the face and the delicate softness of the breasts, arms and abdomen. Dignified and restrained, this beautiful presentation of the river goddess is a masterpiece of Bengali terracotta art and does much credit to the unknown sculptor who wrought it.

PLATE 42 : Gaja-Lakshmi, Charbangla Temple (North), Baranagar, Dist. Murshidabad, West Bengal. This representation of the 'Consecration of Lakshmi', a popular art motif of long standing, may be considered as one of the covering deities (*avarana-devatas*) of the temple. Descended from her earliest prototypes at Bharhut and Sanchi, this 'goddess of prosperity' is seated in the Indian fashion (*virasana*) on a full-blown lotus emerging out of its stem. She is profusely ornamented with the usual items of jewellery, of which particular mention may be made of a *kiritamukuta* on the head and a jewelled *kucha-vandha* securing the breasts. What is very unconventional about her, is that the elephants who are bathing her by pouring water from inverted jars held in their trunks, are not shown as standing on either side, as is usual, but are depicted as held by her in her hands.

PLATE 43 : Mahishasura-mardini, Charbangla Temple (North), Baranagar, Dist. Murshidabad, West Bengal. This image of the ten-handed Mahishasura-mardini is another *avarana-devata* on the walls of the temple. The softness of the plastic modelling, diffused throughout the entire composition, with the exception of the stylized lion with its stiffened limbs and elongated horse-like face, imparts a cosy grace to this otherwise conventional portrayal of a common and popular theme.

PLATE 44 : Annapurna giving alms to Siva, Charbangla Temple (South), Baranagar, Dist. Murshidabad, West Bengal. This panel depicts a popular Saiva legend, which deals with the alms-begging of Siva from Annapurna, one of the numerous names of his divine spouse. Annapurna, seated on the throne is seen dealing out the alms from a bowl held in her right hand to her begger husband who is standing completely naked before her. The whole composition has been pervaded by a comic element through the grotesque, almost clownish, countenances of the actors. The sculptor seems to have followed a popular version of the legend, as embodied in the mediaeval Mangala-kavyas, like the Annada-mangala of Bharata Chandra, which depicts Siva and his wife, not as divine beings, but as common mortal householder and housewife.

PLATE 45 : Krishna dancing with the Gopinis, Madanmohan Temple, Bishnupur, Dist. Bankura, West Bengal. This terracotta plaque, depicting one of his boyish pranks (*bala-lila*), shows Krishna dancing with the Gopinis, one of whom is playing on a drum and another on a pair of cymbals. A flowing lyricism pervades throughout the whole composition and the ecstasy of expression imparts sublimity to it.

PLATE 46 : Terracotta panels depicting the battle between Rama and Ravana, Joydev Temple, Joydev Kenduli, Dist. Birbhum, West Bengal. These panels depict the epic battle of Rama, helped by his simian followers, against Ravana, the lord of a numerous Rakshasa host. The uppermost panel shows Rama and Lakshmana, mounted on chariots, shooting arrows at their adversary, the ten-headed king of Lanka, who stands fully armed in front of them. The other panels below show the monkey hordes, some of whom are armed with uprooted trees and others with huge boulders of rock, giving battle to the Rakshasa legions. In the middle of each of these panels, the opposing forces are seen engaged in hand to hand grapple. In the extreme right of the third panel from above, a Rakshasa soldier is seen devouring a monkey. The simian pranks of the monkeys and the demoniac orgy of the Rakshasas gives a somewhat comic effect to this heroic scene.

PLATE 47 : Terracotta panels showing scenes from the Ramayana, Surul Temple, Surul, Dist. Birbhum, West Bengal. These panels deal with the episodes connected with Hanumana's search for Sita. The lowermost panel shows Sita in the Asoka grove of Lanka being tormented by the she-goblins (*chedis*) of Ravana's entuorage, some of whom are counselling her to take Ravana to husband, while others are maltreating her for refusing their request. The monkey-chief who has just found her in the grove, is seen espying her perching on the branches of a tree on the extreme right of the panel. The middle panel shows Ravana, enthroned in his court, remonstrating with his brother Vibishana for his good councils. The uppermost panel depicts the battle between the Rakshasa legions of Ravana and Hanumana prior to his burning the golden city of Lanka. The sensitive lyricism of the Asoka-vana scene, contrasting heavily with regal grandeur of the court-scene and the action and movement of the battle scene, endows variety and relief to these panels.

PLATE 48 : Terracotta panels depicting the battle between Rama and Ravana, Surul Temple, Surul, Dist. Birbhum, West Bengal. These panels, like those illustrated in plate 46, depict the Ramayanic battle between Rama and Ravana. The heroic temper of the struggle, with all the bustle and fury of an epic battle, has been very truthfully portrayed in the action and movement of the combatants, which imparts an epic greatness to this scene.

PLATE 49 : Terracotta panels showing scenes from the Ramayana, Surul Temple, Surul, Dist. Birbhum, West Bengal. The lowermost panel possibly depicts the leave-taking of Rama, Lakshmana and Sita from their parents on the eve of the departure from Ayodhya on exile for fourteen years. The middle panel shows Rama with Sita enthroned in open *darbar*, attended by his half-brothers, Bharata (holding the umbrella), Lakshmana and Satrughna (waving chamaras) and his simian councillors, Hanumana and Jambuvana and others, after his return from Lanka. The uppermost panel depicts the performance of the *Asvamedha* (?) sacrifice by Rama. The portrayal of Sita in *darbar* scene as an ordinary Bengali housewife, drawing the veil over her face is noteworthy.

PLATE 50 : Terracotta panels depicting the battle between Rama and Ravana, Palpara Temple, Chakdah, Dist. Nadia, West Bengal. Like plates 46 and 48, this is also a depiction of the battle of Rama and Ravana. The somewhat stiffened plastic treatment of the modelling detracts much from the action and movement of the scene. The epic greatness of this scene, however, consists in its panoramic vastness and depth.